Where Babylon Ends

TO MY WEST

Cape Goliard

Nathaniel Tarn

Where Babylon Ends

COPYRIGHT (C) 1967 NATHANIEL TARN

STANDARD BOOK NUMBER 206.61388.1 PAPER
206.61389.X CLOTH
LIBRARY OF CONGRESS NUMBER 68-15649

Where Babylon Ends

'*Nec Babylonios temptaris numeros*'

Where Babylon ends
no one knows now.

I'd like before the world is ripe
to make men cry for what they are
once and for all so that
they never cry again
and this old top
stops spinning—
for then we can begin

to clarify the city,
to build with bricks you know
tall cliffs of fiery letters
far, far from Babylon
to touch the thunder's lips—
but where Babylon ends
no one knows now.

I am Hebrew they say,
i.e. I do not understand
the gambler's spinning wheel,
the rules of wanton chance,
raps on the knuckles for Jupiter's triplets,
the sag in each thread of our lives:
art for art's sake.

It may be true. It may be true.
Where they preach this, in any case:
silence. With us, a generation gone,
the ache of standstill
and then quite suddenly
the recovered gasp
of the teaching breath.

Now lights will flash on
and off in quick succession.
Flat on your bellies you will be amazed
by simple things
violently lit, then occulted.
Leave labyrinths to birds and moles
who brook no obstacles

but men wish clear well-water.
In the cracks of Babylon
willows grow
where light awakes.
I rise to the holy Jerusalem of all angels
and speak to you in those provinces
she has in every nook and cranny of your countries.

The Winter Princes

The wind drops beasts down the chimneys,
the winter roars about his head
muffled in the stone zoos.

How easily contracted
this illness love!
Licked into life again
the furry heart
like a reluctant bear cub.
But if the boy god stays,
if he stores his arrows mind you,
it won't be for a long time yet
and he'll let the Mayor know first
and the Mayor will let you know.

Where his country's arms
with their river bracelets
lose fields awash
on a sweat of wheat,
where the sun bleeds
the raven white
and the dove chars
at a touch of sky,
where he will never go, never adventure,
his love glows in her sleep.

While every friend
warms a surburban house
from which he goes to work,
to which he comes at evening,
within which no one meets—
cries for an ark of animals
led by his younger self,
handsome in chains of office—
crying each one inside,
silent and bitter.

She too, and in the deluge of her sleep.

After the Roaring Forties

Waking at midnight:
the sudden meanness of
confronted clay.
No wind to flatten faces
against this skull—
faces the captain wears
when he is not
captain but each in turn
his shallow crew.
Death is the matter where
this storm has stilled
a soothing passage for
his residue of life.
Persuade *this* one he fails
to move for lack of conflict!
He does not wish to hail
other ships passing
or stealing home
back to their mother ports,
bellows no questions
at the sky, nor begs
news of white whale or black
the sea for all he knows renews
each day out of her ovaries;
he does not ask
of albatross or petrel
his fodder's destinations,
follows no tern
to garden islands
tilled by blue breakers.
Still grows his age
cored with the stricken sun,
tall, in the sea's clenched fist,
sun, passage, water, all
weaned of their questions.

A Head and a Lyre in Water

To Eurydice:
Certain that I would never be given,
never be granted that beauty,
such beauty as wheeled the world
when the rocks ran together
to crush our weaving ship,
yet they conspired to give her to me
who am no hero,
but only makes animals grieve
they have no tongues to sing with,
yet I master that beauty
and bless it with each of my limbs
as they float down to Lesbos.

And again to Eurydice:
if you ever float out of my reach,
that is: if I die now altogether,
bereaved of heart and mind
and the voice to praise you with—
beware, beware I haunt you
in the wet leaf underfoot,
the crest of light you swim,
the moth on the air you breathe—
generation after generation
while you attempt to forget
I shall come back at you
singing the same old words:
it is an old, old story
that you must recognize,
my name is spelt like Orpheus,
yours like Eurydice.

And again to Eurydice:
my head lodged among rocks
behind my lyre's bars
I leave the myriad things
you are compounded of
that will not come together again.
Your turn to turn has come
though the lyre deny it always,
I melting out of Orpheus,
you turning like a ship,
bearing away the fleece,
never a passenger again
in your own hold.

And again to Eurydice:

The Five Senses

"According to the mixture that each man has in his wandering limbs, so thought is forthcoming to mankind; for that which thinks is the same thing, namely the substance of their limbs, in each and all men; for that of which there is more is thought."
                              Parmenides of Elea

Bone level reached,
the forehead of the earth:
the earth's a skull,
its senses lost in space.
We are its mind
collectively,
so many cells
whose work is hunger,
whose every rift
is like an inquisition.
Below: a bridal veil
of long nerves falls,
medusas in the void,
deader to pain than hair.

As one about to break
with birth whose legs are tied
is laboured by the thrust
of the whole world arrested
above a membrane crust
of frozen milk:
she holds the earth to ransom:
tree-twigs and beaks of birds,
fish-fins, crab-claws and pincers,
shin-bones of animals,
elbows of infants,
craving for definition.
A tide over the heart
thaws her milk to blood.

I thought, she said,
you were a creature also
of the night. And lived
much more than most men do
in your five senses.

Ah no, I said, a daylight mind
this decomposing world
exacerbates to act.
But look, she said, look here:
this infant love I've made—
my legs untied—he sings
like a dawn chorus. I think
to live, I said, and nervously
tangled the vocals in his throat.

Language has done with me
whose senses lived at all
only while here and now
implied before and after.
Sit here on the still world,
wave here I used to say:
a commonwealth of effort
maintains this thinking globe
in its illusive courses,
and what the day unravels
the night will weave again
into selected patterns
all can decipher. Now, no,
I cannot scan, can hardly utter.

Can't you accept, she asked,
love, now the mind's at bay
and lie at peace with me
breeding our children?
Can't we say yes at last
and let our seed flow free
unhindered by your laws
and skeletons of order?
We fold this life in half,
meet on its edges. Were mind

to fade, our senses could agree,
our speech remember us,
recite our blood together,
paying one quittance in one currency.

Markings

Un homme se possède par éclaicies, et même quand il se possède, il ne s'atteint pas tout à fait.
                                        Antonin Artaud

My writing to forget
the thing I love
is but the signature
a root of fire
(that always seeks a home
but cannot find
a residence to let
and rise into)
must mark with to endure.
I sign with scent of breath,
with body rub,
against your willing flanks
so that remembrances
renew themselves till death,
project through history
intra-specific thanks
white skin by skin.
The game of win and lose
being but lick and sniff
we go as dogs progress
from sin to perfumed sin,
lifting a leg to trace
along your bare midriff
the sign of the true way.
Or when the doves digress
to build in bridal air
their parodies of grace
our feet race on below
with the black hound of hell
and resurrection's hare.
Where there's no stop and go
a thought may wet your face,
a breath arrest your stare.

Look: everything forgets
in this pure atmosphere—
before the sunshine sets
or the bright air can die,
it's time to make a start,
and mark in memory
these rituals of art.

The Novice

The grass had grown again
my animals could graze on.
I had declared the herds,
my love had bared
her breasts like pastures.
Along her skin
the light ran wild like lambs,
the summer winds swelled in her hair.
My fields danced in the sun,
orchards exploded.

I walked with human love as I had not
ever believed that human love could be,
spoke quietly her praise
whose body sang the earth's,
lay still, lay very still
inside my heart
for fear my life escape
to run again like wolves
along the forest rim,
contriving murder.

The moon inhaled her tides:
the earth's blood froze.
Good God what shall I do
with the new grass now charred
and cut again under my very feet?
The earth's black floor—
these fields we tilled together,
stripped of their produce—
gapes like a trap
I fall through to my eyes.

My pastures turn and sour under the moon,
night owns them altogether.
Familiar ghosts break from their lairs
to roam the land on stilts,
grazing dream ceilings.
Fanged like the adult wolf,
they lock the fields in packs,
worry along the snow
the he-goat to his knees,
the sheep to her white sides.

The birds have died of grief
on withered branches
and all the surge of summer
has shrunk in them.
I have aged in a single day
beyond my understanding,
my hair has lost its sheen,
my bones their marrow—
yet I am still a cub, cannot achieve
the rapt proficiency of a grown wolf.

Her face is barking mad,
her eyes have made me retch
and vomit leaks its acid in my throat.
In depths where I was spawned
her promiscuity
has bitten bane and blood-rust.
Can wounds discuss themselves with knives,
their lips frame such a conversation?
And how shall fangs
ever square back to her white teeth again?

But to forget, or to obliterate
her smile in rage: that also sickens.
Perhaps I go, perhaps I leave her,
perhaps I let the colours drain
down the world's spine, the blood ebb back
through interrupted sources—
perhaps I cease to talk
with the one voice that made my voice my own
since she was all that cast my husbandry
like seed into the furrows of the sky.

Perhaps I go, perhaps I leave her,
bitch among wolves,
her heat drawing the packs
more than the blood of prey—
perhaps the cub allows
the grey, ascendant lords
to keep her gross rump down.
With boundless charity
she sheathes and holds their blades
in swelling stupor.

We shall grow old together, she and I,
our enmities grown old,
on sundered continents.
From time to time a girl with her dead eyes
will loose the cubs of summer
to jolt my evening brain.
Letters will cross, written in two dead hands,
still measuring partitions in the tides.
Purged of a passion which had dwarfed my life,
I shall attempt, at last, to take my vows.

For Mahler

A surf of cradles on the sea as far as the eye reaches.

And look your triremes moving in the wind, your violins,
violas, cellos, the galley slaves leaning to the wind,
and the oars obeying, laid in one wind like a cornfield,
one row of oars circling, curving, so, and the others
soaring above the surf of cradles, the driven snow.

Slowly, infinitesimally, you raise your church of icebergs,
your stone by stone storm, ice vaults, whalebone arches,
with a child's bone pinned in the spire's spine,
the wind like a melody crying mother, mother, mother,
as you come by, old architect, with nothing but hands.

High where the air is rare and where the breath falls,
dips like a gull over the lungs, where the sea birds
are hands, so many hands, some curved, the others soaring,
your elevations faltering on those heights, those triremes
hardly knowing where they are any more, and the flowers:

Look the roses the oars have sown in sombre sea furrows,
dear Jew, dry sperm of Sinai dissolved in polar streams:
you have put roses in death's sea where nothing ever thrived,
billows like mothers' breasts over the surf of cradles,
your mouth begins to frame the cry no one could cry.

The muscles of a towering old man with desperate hands,
a polar bear dancing to tin whistles, to trumpets,
juggling before his Virgin with inexpressible concepts,
whopping his testicles, smelting in liquid sulphur
unalterable Zion's walls circled about with icebergs!

The cradles grind each other and the babes die. And the babes
die, Gustav Mahler, for lack of larchwood in the cold,

for lack of bread and milk and coverings,
while we lie lulled and frosted among flowers—
and I ask you: do we break their hearts before our songs

break ours, or are we home, mein Lieber, safely in Vienna?

Eagle Hunt, Hidatsa Indians, U.S.A.

An eagle on the air, an
acrobat on the air's high wires, with an ascetic's attention,
ceaselessly back to its line, back to itself,
mind balanced in waiting for prey,
hovers above the furrows

lining a giant's face—
where time has no beads of sweat to tell, the sun no longer spins,
the tides have no waters to move, the moon
no waves to heave among the seas
and every breath of air pays attention:

where whatever moves falls prey to the stillness,
gored in the talons of that patience,
and is promised to death with a sigh,
without even a feather's hiss
in the hush of arrows.

And the hunter too, drowned in his loam,
sunk in the leaves and twigs of his trap,
aches for the child-boned throat
his fingers will crack with a sound of wood
crushed underfoot by deerskin in the forest.

The bird does not fall easy to his grasp—
the seeming hunter to the seeming prey—
that patience will not plummet out of the sky for so little,
for the sake of two hands tipped with sleep.
The bird is drawn down by the hunter's wife

bleeding her month out over the leaves
where autumn rots in the rusting woods.
She'd be locked at home if this were earth-hunting.
But to distill that stillness from the sky,
to close the distance between bird and man,

there is need of the bait she bleeds, the earth's decay.
Down flock the feathers: the eagle comes
seeming to pluck the lure. This death occurs as we collapse in dreams.
The great wings fold and close and no one counts
how many fingers brought the sky down.

From wingtip to wingtip the earth basked in their grasp
and league spoke to league without let or hindrance.
The fathers hovered on the feathered corn
spilling the seasons in their marriage dance:
prey moved in and out of the shadows at legitimate speed.

The nights were scalped by eagles' claws, the trophies gleamed.

The Laurel Tree

Streamed in her thirty-third year as i surmise this girl of rivers
uncertain whether back or forward to flow the present difficult
poured where two seas fight shy of mingling
thrust through the midst of them and parted them and rose
clothed in no clothes and without ornament
onto the beach of this lemon country

     turtle as ageless as her sorrow stones
     lays amber from her eyes as her eggs fall
     turns to inhale the sea so she believes
     but follows death inland
     melts in her carapace

ironed to wafers by the sky
this is the sand-pan greased with oil
the only dent in mile on mile of beach
into which she fitted the shape of her beautiful years
we outsweated the sun on that day and nearly drowned each other
doing nothing beyond that to spice love

     tarantula lies with a stake through her loins
     her legs curl like the planets round the sun
     she slowly sails the day as if at ease
     her eggs meanwhile as bloodshot as the salmon's
     although unnatural

she washed the foam from her hair in the whipping waters
fulfilled her needs invisibly in the sea
stood up in a surf of salt-bleached dolls
came over to brood me where i lay in the thyme
the bees in her breasts wove the thrashing gorse
her down her mandorla of light

       a messenger yes/no a semaphore
       her black/white keys her in/out whirl of morse
       hoopooe signals salvation deviously
       closed are the doors of death by thy donations
       in the bowl of her wings she awaits our alms

since when i have looked for her as far as the earth is pleased to turn
to make the ships glide by as if they did not move
with wings at their funnels and resounding names
since when i have brushed every inch of the earth with sunlight
to etch her out of her landscape who had fled from me
turning to fibre behind her navel my hot seed

            suffering servants now
            are black and smell and do not smile
            they do not remain human very long when
                looked at
            their children's chins are smelted to their chests
            even a mother is at pains to love

she is turning to wood in my arms at the knot in her knees
the branches in her thighs the boughs from breasts to armpits
she is turning to wood in the hot furrow of her belly
where it curves to meet the crease under her spine
she is turning to wood between her lips she cannot talk
she is turning to wood along her fingers they will bear leaves

            children unborn dream of lemons
            flies suck the furrows in their faces
            parched skin cracks
            on certain sections the skin turns inside out
            garbage in newspapers

as for the gathering in of her desires as for her age
should no one even look at us in the streets any more as we pass
it is a long time none the less since we have been alone in joy
or since there has been a possibility of anything in our lives but joy
and yet though grateful for each other's coincidence at this time
we are happiness-blind

                      a year has died since that blue sky
                      since the wound in her fur hung with pearls
                      a sparrow nestles in the crook of a branch
                      we do not see the burning flesh behind it
                      it is essence of bird essence of love

grow to wood   lose your silks   develop habits   but do not leave
this servant who would lie and drift by you his worthless life
i call her gaze to prolong the branches
shape to the wind if there be any wind where we have been
wake oh my suffering hands upon your suffering hands·
let them fall with the leper's thumb into the bowl out of our means

Projections for an Eagle Escaped in this City, March 1965

AND HOW I BARE YOU ON EAGLES' WINGS

Towards the poem
as towards
any winter initiative,
fatigue cubes effort.
To be evil is nothing but to be tired,
selling short takes little more than to be weary,
those born to stumble claim no redress.
        Wrong done to them
            is wrong in general.

SO THE STRUCK EAGLE STRETCHED UPON THE PLAIN

To have swept upwards
past startled hands, past
frightened fingers, past bars, past
the idea of liberty even,
to have swept up
out of his iron Egypt, this winter day
was this coincidence?
        By acting now on the external world
        and changing it,
        he at the selfsame time
        changes his nature.

OFFICIOUS HASTE DID LET TOO SOON THE SACRED EAGLE FLY

In the prison
of the underworld,
in Sheol (Tropicana),
their spectrum of colours
spreads the radiance of Egypt
for the golden bull
and his spangled heifer.
           In the 19th century,
           from Bogota, Colombia,
           millions of hummers p.a.
           One London firm alone:
           400,000 corpses
           plucked for adornment.

FOR WHERESOEVER THE CARCASE IS THERE WILL THE EAGLES BE GATHERED TOGETHER

Though the people do not even flock to their king.
It is enough that the king rules again
wingtip to wingtip spanning the upper air
and clouding the nether air with his shadow.
All those these walls enthrall, while more
than mathematic gloom envelops all around,
peer up from city windows and compute
the king's position in the famished skies.

The gates of Sheol
open on corridors
which open onto light
in this our world. But that illusion,
quantum of darkness in the rush of light,
bars hummers from the knowledge of their freedom.
Egypt is weariness of heart. Specifications of
        319 Apodiformes Trochilidae:
        flight muscles forming
        some 25% of body weight,
        unique wingbone to shoulder swiveljoint
        permits wingplane adjustment to the air.
        55 wingbeats per second in hoverflight,
        75 w.p.s. in level flight. Courtship:
        (O as for U-loop love-buzz) 200 w.p.s.

    SKYWARD IN AIR A SUDDEN MUFFLED SOUND THE
                                     DALLIANCE OF THE EAGLES

While the king has not learned his trade.
Who shall, from the holarctic rim, in legions,
as in the days of Aquila Chrysaëtos, hoist in Rome,
bate bearing crowns and sceptres in their pinions,
lightning in talons, the blizzard in their tails,
flutter'd your Volscians in Corioli,
and teach to kill? and teach to wind
the kingdom out on ever widening orbits?

The list of his Majesty's subjects
in his provinces of latter-day Egypt:
Cuban Bee, Calypte Helenae, $2\frac{1}{4}$ in., Isle of Pines.
Frilled Coquette, Lophornis Magnifica, $2\frac{3}{4}$ in., Brazil.
Adorable Coquette, Paphosia Adorabilis, 3 in., Costa Rica.

Popelaire's Thornbill, Popelairia Popelairii, 4½ in., Ecuador.
Violet Sabrewing, Campylopterus Hemileucurus, 5 in., Mexico-
                                                          Panama.
Collared Inca, Coeligena Torquata, 5¼ in., Colombia-Peru.
Sappho Comet, Sappho Sparganura, 7 in., Bolivia.
Greentailed Sylph, Aglaiocercus Kingi, 7½ in., Andes.
Crimson Topaz, Topaza Pella, 7½ in., Guianas.
Streamertail, Trochilus Polytmus, 9½ in., Island of Jamaica.
            And others as per itemized list attached.

Here in Sheol
by skeletal willows,
by ghostly streams,
their exiled harps are hung.
They doze in hibernation by the hour.
Their king has gone out of bondage from Egypt,
Babylon, Spain, New Spain and all the Russias.
            Ring'd with the azure world, he stands.
            And the best of merry luck to him.

THAT WITH HIS SHARPE LOK PERSETH THE SONNE

While the king has not learned his trade.
He addresses, fratres, the flannelled crowd, Romani,
the keepers and dogs, populares, he addresses,
the city truants, workers, the photographers, of the world,
the journalists, unite, he addresses, the Sunday idle,
every valley, scorning the ladders, shall be exalted,
or baited lures, and every mountain shall be laid low,
the other dainty captives brought to tempt him,
he addresses, comfort ye, his tormentors, comfort ye,
dropping away, my people, with one flap of his leathers.

Towards Sheol
as towards
a fear to find, within the body's watch,
the jewelled bone responsibility,
they are content, in cages wide as breath,
wide as breath only, to spring the adequate
and whip their whirring wings from sip to song.
    Crests, fans, tufts, wires, pendants and
    pantaloons, shields, gorgets, whiskers
    and iridescent plumage. Nature
    plus History will shortly be as one.

THE WRENS MAKE PREY WHERE EAGLES DARE NOT PERCH

Beyond these walls, this stone circumference,
lie his enthusiasms, snow-pure, untampered with,
ready to leap-frog time. Which, born in slavery,
he has not learned to scan. Here where the earth is glue
and feeds but stubble he dreams an Israel,
the rocks and crags on which he builds his nest,
the hearth of cedars where he plants his banners,
the dove-grey prey so hot of blood, the sun
crazing the day, the soothing moon,
the taloned stars: Sheol in splinters.

The hummer never walks or climbs. Feet are
for perching only. Metabolism rate
being so high, migrations of
500 miles would call
for subcutaneous fuel loads
adding 50% to body weight
before the Exodus.

Lab. tests have proved
such feats impossible.
Yet hummers could
back in their days of Nature,
before the massacres and slaughters
(tears of the Indies),
perform it nonetheless twice every year.

THAT IS THE HUM-BIRD NOT MUCH EXCEEDING A BEETLE

Wherefore the king, as all such stories end, will learn
his trade. His shadow magnifies the swelling land,
stooping to prey grown fat on idleness.
He has gone to Pharaoh, who said No. He has decided Yes.
He has worked out that frontiers concern subjects
who may rot in their colours and emblems if they will.
He will shift continents, change poles, night into day, day, night.
Freeze deserts, make of the sands his snows.
Fire the snows, renew himself in ice.
Quit his armies if need be and resign after Canaan.

Though the city change coin into weapons, and ingots
to instruments of war, his lungs will flower, his heart
bear fruit. Mounting up with wings as a storm cloud, unafraid.
That the seas may not run dry, nor the rivers falter.

Burying his right wing in orchards and vineyards
against the whirlwind bred on Sinai,
honey lapped from a lion gut, milk from the mouths of lambs,
men lie with beaks and talons, marrow for talismans,

*where they shall not fear, naked bone, but for him in his air,
in this crucible's fire, a throne, a torch of spices—
in the fan of his wings now, his resurrected voice,
the assent of these palms, in this wind, peace,*

nor shall there be slaves here any more. Peace. Selah. Poem. Amen.

Acknowledgments are made to: Agenda, Ambit, Flourish, Penguin Modern Poets No. 7, Quest, Solstice, The Spectator, "A Tribute to Hugh MacDiarmid on his 75th Birthday", Unicorn Folios, and the B.B.C. Third Programme.

BY THE SAME AUTHOR

OLD SAVAGE/YOUNG CITY, London & New York
SELECTION: PENGUIN MODERN POETS No. 7
THE HEIGHTS OF MACCHU PICCHU: translated from the Spanish of Pablo Neruda, London & New York.

This first edition was Designed, Printed & Published by Cape Goliard Press Ltd 10a Fairhazel Gardens, London N.W.6. March 1968;
& consists of 2,700 copies: 2,000 soft cover, 700 case bound, of which 50 are signed & numbered by the author.
1,400 copies of this edition have been printed for joint publication in the United States by Richard Grossman Inc., New York.

Printed in Great Britain